TABLE OF CONTENTS

Essential Oil Cooking Conversion Chart	1
About Essential Oils	2
Cooking Tip Chart	7
Appetizers	8
Beverages	16
Breakfast	30
Main Dishes	36
Edible Extras	68
Vegetables	78
Slow Cooker	88
Side Dishes	100
Desserts	116

ESSENTIAL OIL COOKING CONVERSION CHART

ESSENTIAL OIL	HERB/SPICE
1 spoon swirl Black Pepper essential oil*	1/2 teaspoon black pepper spice
1 teaspoon Basil essential oil	1 teaspoon dried basil leaves
1 drop Cinnamon essential oil	1 teaspoon ground cinnamon
1 drop Clove essential oil	1/2 teaspoon ground clove spice
1 spoon swirl Dill essential oil*	2 teaspoons fresh dill
1 drop Ginger essential oil	1/4 teaspoon ground ginger
1 drop Grapefruit essential oil	1 teaspoon grapefruit zest
1 drop Lemon essential oil	1 teaspoon lemon zest
1 drop Lime essential oil	1 teaspoon lime zest
1 drop Nutmeg essential oil	1 teaspoon dried nutmeg spice
1 drop Orange essential oil	1 teaspoon orange zest
1 drop Oregano essential oil	1 teaspoon oregano spice
1 drop Peppermint essential oil	1/2 teaspoon dried peppermint leaves
1 drop Rosemary essential oil	1/2 teaspoon rosemary spice
1 drop Sage essential oil	1 teaspoon sage spice
1 drop Tangerine essential oil	1 teaspoon tangerine zest
1 drop Thyme essential oil	1 teaspoon thyme spice

*See About Essential Oils page for delivery method.

I only recommend ingesting 100% Certified Pure Therapeutic Grade essential oils. To order visit www.edibleessentialoils.com.

About Essential Oils

Essential oils have powerful therapeutic healing properties. Not only can they effect emotions and assist in healing physical ailments, the possibilities of creativity in the kitchen are endless. Essential oils are highly concentrated, and are 50-70% more potent than herbs.

Edible essential oils must be obtained from a pure source. Over 95% of essential oils on the market are not pure, and are not suitable for ingestion. **I only recommend ingesting 100% Certified Pure Therapeutic Grade essential oils. To order visit www.edibleessentialoils.com.**

DELIVERY OPTIONS:

SPOON SWIRL METHOD:

Tip the bottle slowly until a drop begins to form. Take a spoon and touch the end of the partial drop. Swirl the spoon into the liquid ingredients you are using in your recipe (i.e. a spoon swirl mixed with olive oil).
This is similar to the toothpick technique (dipping a toothpick into the bottle), but I prefer using the spoon swirl technique since the toothpick absorbs some of the oil, and I want to mix as much of the flavor as possible into the ingredients.

DROP METHOD:

You can add the drops of oil directly from the bottle to your liquid ingredients (i.e. adding basil oil to spaghetti sauce). I still add the drop onto a spoon, and stir it in. Some oils come out of the bottle faster than others. For instance, if a recipe calls for 1 drop of oregano oil and 2 drops come out of the bottle the oil can overpower the dish. Oils of a citrus nature would be more forgiving if you were to add an additional drop to the mixture.

BASIL OIL

Most commonly used in cooking, this appetizing oil can infuse your favorite recipes with its aroma and flavor. Add a few drops to any dish and experience the benefits of essential oils baked right into your favorite meals. Inhaling basil can refresh the mind and restores mental alertness, and may also sharpen your sense of smell.

BLACK PEPPER

Black pepper has a pungent, crisp aroma that is comforting and energizing. It is supportive of the digestive system and is useful topically for soothing muscle discomfort following exercise.

CINNAMON

The warm, spicy aroma of cinnamon has been sought throughout the ages both as a valuable commodity and for its ability to improve wellness. Cinnamon is meticulously tested to ensure that no dilution from similar smelling oils has occurred. Cinnamon is thought to promote healthy cardiovascular and immune function, and acts as an antiseptic.

CLOVE

Clove has a sweet, spicy fragrance that is stimulating and revitalizing. With wonderful immune enhancing properties, its principal constituent is eugenol, which is used in the dental industry to numb the gums. Clove is the highest scoring single ingredient ever tested for its antioxidant capacity on the ORAC (Oxygen Radical Absorbance Capacity) scale. Always dilute for topical use.

DILL

Dill oil has a spicy, fresh scent that is stimulating, revitalizing, and balancing. Use dill essential oil for cooking or preparing food to enhance flavor.

GINGER

Ginger has a warm, spicy fragrance that is energizing. Supportive of the digestive system, ginger is commonly used to soothe, comfort, and balance digestive discomfort.

GRAPEFRUIT

Grapefruit has a fresh, citrus aroma that is energizing and uplifting. Rich in the powerful antioxidant d-limonene, it is nourishing to the skin. Like many cold pressed citrus oils, it is a popular oil to use in conjunction with weight management programs.

LEMON

Lemon has a strong, purifying, citrus scent that is revitalizing and uplifting. Lemon consists of 68% d-limonene, a powerful antioxidant. It is delightfully refreshing in water and may be beneficial for the skin. Lemon may also be used to enhance the flavor of foods. Lemon essential oil is cold-pressed from the rinds of lemons.

LIME

Lime essential oil has an invigorating and stimulating effect and is believed to be native of eastern Malaysia. The pleasant citrus aroma of lime may help mental clarity and encourage creativity. Today, lime is best known throughout the world as a way to help support a healthy immune system, and may help aid in weight management.

NUTMEG

Nutmeg has a sweet, warm, spicy scent similar to the spice commonly used in cooking. Comforting and soothing, nutmeg helps boost energy. It also supports nervous and endocrine systems and prostaglandin balance.

ORANGE

Orange essential oil has a rich, fruity scent that lifts the spirit while providing a calming influence on the body. Orange oil brings peace and happiness to the mind. It is rich in the powerful antioxidant d-limonene and aids in maintaining normal cellular regeneration.

OREGANO

Oregano is one of the most powerful and versatile essential oils. It contains strong immune-enhancing and antioxidant properties and supports the respiratory system.

PEPPERMINT

Peppermint has a strong, clean, fresh, minty aroma. One of the oldest and most highly regarded herbs for soothing digestion; it may also restore digestive efficiency. Jean Valnet, M.D., studied peppermint's supportive effect on the liver and respiratory systems. Other scientists have also researched peppermint's role in improving taste and smell when inhaled. Dr. William N. Dember of the University of Cincinnati studied peppermint's ability to improve concentration and mental sharpness. Alan Hirsch, M.D., studied peppermint's ability to directly affect the brain's satiety center, which triggers a sensation of fullness after meals.

ROSEMARY

Rosemary has a fresh, herbaceous, sweet, slightly medicinal aroma. An energizing oil, it may be beneficial for helping to restore mental alertness when experiencing fatigue.

SAGE

Sage has a spicy, herbaceous aroma. It has been recognized for its ability to strengthen the senses and vital centers of the body and to support metabolism. It is helpful for supporting the respiratory, reproductive, nervous, and other body systems. Sage may help in coping with despair and mental fatigue.

TANGERINE

Tangerine is a calming essential oil with a sweet, tangy aroma, similar to orange. It helps with occasional nervous irritability. An excellent oil to help uplift the spirit and bring about a sense of security, tangerine is also rich in the powerful antioxidant d-limonene.

THYME

Thyme has a spicy, warm, herbaceous aroma that is both powerful and penetrating. Known since ancient times as a medicinal herb, thyme contains large amounts of thymol. As a dietary supplement, it is one of the strongest antioxidants known. Thyme supports the immune, respiratory, digestive, nervous, and other body systems.

COOKING TIPS CHART

Essential Oil	Strong	Citrus	Subtle	Health Benefits
Basil	✓			Digestive support, respiratory relief, uplifts mood
Black Pepper	✓			Anti-bacterial, diuretic, anti-arthritic
Cinnamon	✓			Circulatory support, respiratory relief, regulates blood sugar
Clove			✓	Stress relief, headache relief, blood circulation
Dill	✓			Sedative, digestive support, anti-anxiety
Fennel	✓			Diuretic, headache relief, cough expectorant
Ginger	✓			Circulation support, digestive aid, anti-inflammatory
Grapefruit		✓		Metabolic stimulant, anti-oxidant, anti-depressant
Lavender			✓	Insomnia relief, pain relief, immunity booster, calming
Lemon		✓		Assist in weight loss, immune booster, treats asthma
Lime		✓		Anti-depressant, anti-fungal, restorative tonic
Marjoram	✓			Anti-viral, diuretic, calming, sedative
Nutmeg	✓			Regulates blood pressure, heart support, pain relief
Orange		✓		Anti-inflammatory, uplifts mood, sedative
Oregano	✓			Anti-viral, anti-bacterial, anti-fungal, immune support
Peppermint	✓			Stimulant, digestive support, relives nausea
Rosemary	✓			Boost mental activity, pain relief, digestive support
Spearmint	✓			Stimulant, restorative tonic, anti-spasmodic
Tangerine		✓		Sedative, boosts immune system, anti-septic
Tarragon	✓			Circulatory support, digestive, boost mental activity
Thyme	✓			Heart support, diuretic, cough expectorant
Wintergreen	✓			Anti-arthritic, stimulant, diuretic

For cooking tips visit www.edibleessentialoils.com

I only recommend ingesting 100% Certified Pure Therapeutic Grade essential oils. To order visit www.edibleessentialoils.com.

Appetizers

Lemon Parmesan Roasted Chickpeas

2 cups canned chickpeas,
   drained

1 tablespoon olive oil

1 clove garlic, minced

1 drop lemon essential oil

1/8 cup parmesan cheese,
   grated

Dash of salt and pepper

Preheat the oven to 375 degrees.
Drain the chickpeas and pat dry.
Spread onto a baking sheet and bake
for 45 minutes, or until crunchy.

Combine all other ingredients into a
bowl and toss with the roasted
chickpeas as soon as they come out of
the oven.

My Daddy's Guacamole

4 avocados

2/3 cups fresh salsa

1 1/2 teaspoons garlic salt

1 tablespoon fresh cilantro,
  chopped

1 spoon swirl lemon essential
  oil*

Mix all ingredients together and let chill for 30 minutes. Serve with corn chips.

*See introduction page for delivery method.

Corn and Roasted Red Pepper Salsa

2 cups shoepeg or yellow corn

8 ounce black beans

1/2 cup roasted red peppers, chopped

3/4 cup tomatoes, chopped and seeded

1/4 cup minced green onion

2 tablespoons fresh parsley, finely chopped

2 teaspoons green chilies

2 drops lime essential oil

1 teaspoon lemon juice

2 teaspoons extra-virgin olive oil

1/2 teaspoon salt

1/4 teaspoon black pepper

Whisk together lime essential oil, lemon juice, olive oil, salt, and pepper and set aside. Combine the remaining ingredients into a large bowl. Add the lime essential oil mixture over the corn mixture and toss well. Serve with corn tortilla chips.

Lemon Mediterranean Hummus

2, 15 ounce cans chickpeas,
   drained

2/3 cup sour cream

2 teaspoons fresh garlic, minced

1 drop lemon essential oil

4 teaspoons balsamic vinegar

1/4 cup chopped roasted red
   peppers

1/4 cup fresh parsley, chopped

4 tablespoons kalamata olives,
   chopped

Add all ingredients to a food processor and blend together. Serve with pita bread or fresh veggies.

Black Out Salsa

2-3 avocados, diced

1/2 cup green onion, chopped

1 can shoepeg white corn,
   drained

1 can black-eyed peas, drained
   and rinsed

2/3 cups cilantro, diced

1 tomato, seeded and chopped

2/3 cups jicama, chopped

Dressing:

1 drop lemon essential oil

1/4 cup olive oil

2 garlic cloves, minced

2 teaspoons cumin

1 teaspoon salt

1 teaspoon pepper

Put all dressing ingredients in a large bowl and whisk. Add all other ingredients. Toss gently to spread dressing around. Serve with corn chips.

It's a Kick Dip

1, 16 ounce carton sour cream

2, 7 ounce cans diced green
  chilies, drained

1/4 cup fresh cilantro, chopped

1/4 cup salsa

2 cloves garlic, minced

1 teaspoon chili powder

5 drops tabasco

3 drops lime essential oil

1/2 teaspoon salt

Combine all ingredients in a large mixing bowl. Cover and chill overnight. Serve with tortilla chips, crackers or an assortment of vegetables.

Beverages

Ginger Snap Smoothie

2 cups pineapple chunks

1/2 papaya chunks

1 pear, sliced

1/2 cup sweet potato chunks

1 drop ginger essential oil

Combine ingredients into a juice blending machine.

Pumpkin Pie Smoothie

1/2 cup pumpkin puree

1 ripe medium-sized banana

1 cup non-fat vanilla frozen
  yogurt

1/2 teaspoon pumpkin pie spice

1 spoon swirl cinnamon
  essential oil*

1/4 teaspoon vanilla extract

1/2 cup crushed ice

1/2 teaspoon agave nectar

Mix all the ingredients in a blender. Top with a sprinkle of cinnamon.

*See introduction page for delivery method.

Berry Chia Smoothie

1/4 cup blueberries

1/4 cup strawberries

1 nectarine, sliced

1 drop tangerine essential oil

1 teaspoon chia seeds

1 cup spinach

Splash of pomegranate juice

Mix all the ingredients in a blender.

Orange Creamsicle Smoothie

1 ripe banana, peeled and sliced

1 tablespoon vanilla extract

3/4 cup orange juice

3/4 cup vanilla Greek yogurt

2 drops orange essential oil

Mix all the ingredients in a blender until thick and creamy.

Apple Pie Smoothie

1 large apple, chopped

1/2 cup unsweetened rice or
   almond milk

1 drop cinnamon essential oil

3/4 cup vanilla Greek yogurt

1 teaspoon chia seeds

1 teaspoon maple syrup

1/4 teaspoon pumpkin pie spice
   or nutmeg

1/4 cup dry oatmeal

Mix all the ingredients in a blender
until thick and creamy.

Tropical Smoothie

1 ripe banana, peeled and sliced

2 drops tangerine essential oil

1/2 cup pineapple chunks

1/2 cup mango chunks

1 cup coconut milk

1 teaspoon organic honey

1/2 cup plain Greek yogurt

1 teaspoon vanilla

1 teaspoon coconut flakes

Mix all the ingredients in a blender until thick and creamy.

Strawberry Shortcake Smoothie

1/2 cup rice milk

2 cups strawberries

1/2 cup dates, chopped

1 cup dry oatmeal

1 tablespoon vanilla

1 spoon swirl nutmeg
   essential oil*

1/2 teaspoon ground cinnamon

Mix all the ingredients in a blender until thick and creamy.

*See introduction page for delivery method.

Raspberry Lemon Smoothie

3/4 cup vanilla Greek yogurt

1/2 cup vanilla rice or almond

  milk

2 drops lemon essential oil

1 cup raspberries

2 teaspoons organic honey

Mix all the ingredients in a blender until thick and creamy.

Blueberry Banana Smoothie

1 ripe banana, peeled and sliced

1 spoon swirl nutmeg

 essential oil*

1 teaspoon vanilla extract

1 cup blueberries

1 tablespoon organic honey

1/4 cup unsweetened rice or

 almond milk

3/4 cup vanilla Greek yogurt

Mix all the ingredients in a blender until thick and creamy.

 *See introduction page for delivery method.

Glorious Green Smoothie

1 ripe banana, peeled and sliced

3/4 cup vanilla Greek yogurt

1 drop lime essential oil

1 1/2 cups spinach leaves

2 teaspoons organic honey

1 green apple

1/2 teaspoon vanilla extract

1/2 cup unsweetened rice or
almond milk

Mix all the ingredients in a blender
until thick and creamy.

St. Patrick's Smoothie

1 cup vanilla Greek yogurt

2 spoon swirls clove
  essential oil*

Dash of ginger powder

1 pear, cored and chopped

1 cup vanilla rice or almond milk

1 cup spinach leaves

1/2 cup parsley

1/2 cup fresh blueberries

4-6 Medjool dates

Mix all the ingredients in a blender until thick and creamy.

*See introduction page for delivery method.

Pom-Pom Iced Tea

4 bags blueberry tea

1 cup POM® juice

2 drops orange essential oil

1/4 teaspoon powdered stevia

(optional)

Bring a pot of water to a boil. Remove from the stove, add the blueberry tea bags and steep for 5 minutes. Pour into a pitcher and stir in the POM juice, 2 drops of orange essential oil and Stevia. Add ice cubes and fill the pitcher to the top with water.

Breakfast

Tangerine Buttermilk Pancakes

2 tablespoons butter

3 drops tangerine essential oil

3/4 teaspoon orange juice

1 1/2 cups flour

2 tablespoons sugar

1 1/2 teaspoon baking powder

1/2 teaspoon baking soda

1/2 teaspoon salt

1 1/2 cups buttermilk

1/4 cup orange juice

1 tablespoon vegetable oil

1 large egg

1 large egg white

Combine first 3 ingredients and set aside. Combine flour and next 4 ingredients in a bowl.

Combine buttermilk, orange juice, oil and 1 egg in a small bowl and whisk together. Add buttermilk mixture to flour mixture and stir until moist. Let stand 15 minutes.

Whisk egg whites until medium peaks form. Fold egg whites into the batter. Preheat griddle to medium heat. Coat pan with cooking spray. Spoon 1/4 cup batter per pancake into griddle. Cook for 3 minutes or until edges begin to bubble and bottom is browned.

Turn pancakes over and cook for 3 minutes or until done. Serve with tangerine butter and syrup. Top with fresh berries (optional).

Baked French Toast Casserole

1 loaf French bread

8 large eggs

2 cups half-and-half

1 cup milk

2 tablespoons sugar

1 teaspoon vanilla extract

1/2 teaspoon pumpkin pie spice

1 spoon swirl nutmeg
   essential oil*

Slice French bread, 1 1/2 inches each. Arrange slices in a generously buttered 9 x 13 inch baking dish (use a deep baking dish, so the topping doesn't bubble over). In a large bowl, combine the remaining 7 ingredients and beat with a beater or whisk until blended. Pour mixture over the bread slices, making sure all are covered evenly with the milk-egg mixture.

Spoon some of the mixture in between the slices. Cover with foil and refrigerate overnight.

Spread praline topping evenly over the bread and bake at 350 degrees for 50 minutes, until puffed and lightly golden.

Praline Topping:

2 sticks butter

1 cup packed light brown sugar

1 cup chopped pecans

2 tablespoons light corn syrup (Karo)

1/2 teaspoon ground cinnamon

1/2 teaspoon ground nutmeg

1 teaspoon maple syrup

Combine all ingredients in a medium bowl and blend well.

*See introduction page for delivery method.

Cinnamon Bread

2, 1-pound packages refrigerated
   pizza dough
1 drop cinnamon essential oil
1 teaspoon pumpkin pie spice
1 cup sugar
8 tablespoons (1 stick) butter,
   melted, plus more for the pan

Heat oven to 375 degrees. Tear off small bits of the dough and roll them into 1 to 1 1/2-inch balls. Place the balls on a plate.

In a small bowl, mix the sugar and pumpkin pie spice together.

Combine the melted butter and cinnamon essential oil. Dip each ball in the butter, then in the sugar mixture. Transfer the balls to a buttered Bundt pan.

Drizzle any remaining butter over the top and sprinkle with any remaining sugar mix. Bake until golden brown, about 40 minutes. Remove from oven and let cool for 5 minutes. Place a plate on top of the pan and carefully flip it over. Tap the bottom to release the bread.

Transfer to a plate and let people pull the bread apart with their fingers

Ginger Apple Muffins

2 cups gluten free baking
   flour

2/3 cup sugar

1 tablespoon baking powder

1/2 teaspoon salt

1 teaspoon ground
   cinnamon

1 spoon swirl clove
   essential oil*

1 teaspoon ground ginger

3/4 cup rice milk

1 cup shredded red apple

1 ripe banana, mashed

1 tablespoon apple cider
   vinegar

1/2 cup crystallized ginger, finely
chopped

Preheat oven to 400 degrees. Use a non-stick muffin pan or line the pan with muffin liners.

In a large mixing bowl, stir together the first seven ingredients.

In a medium mixing bowl, whisk together the remaining ingredients. Add the dry mix to the wet mix and blend well.

Fill muffin cups 3/4 of the way full. Bake at 400 degrees for 20 minutes.

*See introduction page for delivery method.

Banana Bread

1 cup sugar

1/2 cup shortening

2 eggs

1/2 teaspoon vanilla

1 cup very ripe bananas
   (4 medium)

1 spoon swirl nutmeg
   essential oil*

1 1/4 cup flour

1/2 teaspoon salt

3/4 teaspoon baking soda

1 teaspoon cinnamon

1/2 cup walnut halves (optional)

Preheat oven to 350 degrees. In a large mixing bowl, mix together the sugar, shortening, eggs, vanilla and nutmeg essential oil.

In a large ziplock bag, add peeled bananas, seal and smash with fingers (the chunkier, the better). Add bananas to sugar mixture.

In a large bowl, mix the flour, salt, baking soda and cinnamon. Add to banana mixture. Stir well. Add walnuts, if desired, and mix well.

Pour into a bread pan and bake for 40-50 minutes or until a toothpick comes clean when inserted into the middle of the bread.

*See introduction page for delivery method.

Main Dishes

Chicken Marinara

1 1/2 cup chopped spinach

2 egg whites

1/2 cup low fat cottage cheese

1/2 cup ricotta cheese

1/2 cup grated parmesan cheese

3/4 teaspoon garlic powder

3/4 teaspoon ground nutmeg

4 boneless, skinless chicken
    breasts*

1 cup prepared marinara or
    spaghetti sauce

1 drop oregano essential oil

1 drop basil essential oil

Combine spinach with egg whites, cottage cheese, ricotta cheese, parmesan cheese and seasonings. Spread mixture evenly into a 9 x 9 inch baking dish. Place the chicken breasts on top of the spinach mixture. Do not overlap meat.

In a mixing bowl, combine marinara sauce, oregano essential oil and basil essential oil. Mix well. Pour the marinara sauce over the chicken. Sprinkle with parmesan cheese. Bake at 350 degrees for 40 minutes, or until the juice of the chicken in the center runs clear.

*Larger chicken breasts will take longer to cook.

French Prosciutto Chicken

1/4 cup flour or gluten-free flour

1 teaspoon dried thyme

1/2 teaspoon salt

4 skinless, boneless chicken
  breasts, cut in half

1 tablespoon olive oil

5 cups cremini mushrooms, sliced

2 carrots, peeled and sliced,
  1/4" thick

4-5 slices prosciutto

1 cup red wine

1 cup chicken broth

1 tablespoon tomato paste

Combine flour, thyme, and salt in a zip lock bag. Add chicken, seal and shake to coat. Heat a nonstick skillet to medium heat and add the olive oil. Remove the coated chicken from the bag, place in the skillet and brown for 8-10 minutes, turning frequently. Remove the chicken from the pan.

Add the mushrooms, carrots and prosciutto to the pan, and sauté for 3 minutes. Add the wine, chicken broth and tomato paste, and cook 8 minutes.

Return the chicken to the pan and cook for 8 minutes. Serve over polenta, rice or mashed potatoes.

Chipotle Lime Chicken Skewers

1 cup mayonnaise

2 drops lime essential oil

2 tablespoons fresh cilantro, chopped

2 cloves garlic, finely chopped

1 chipotle pepper in adobo sauce, finely chopped

3 large boneless, skinless chicken breasts, cut into bite sized chunks

Combine all ingredients except chicken into a mixing bowl; reserve 1/2 cup mayonnaise mixture. Thread chicken on skewers, then brush with mayonnaise mixture.

Grill chicken, turning once, 9 minutes or until chicken is thoroughly cooked. Serve chicken skewers with reserved mayonnaise mixture.

Ginger Lentil Soup

3 teaspoons olive oil

3 carrots, chopped

1/2 medium onion, chopped

2 teaspoons fresh ginger, peeled
and grated

1 teaspoon minced garlic

1 tablespoon curry powder

1/4 teaspoon salt

1 spoon swirl black pepper
essential oil*

3/4 cup chicken broth

1/4 cup water

1 cup brown lentils, rinsed and
drained

1 tablespoon tomato paste

Heat olive oil in a large saucepan over medium heat. Add carrot and onion; cover and cook 3 minutes or until softened. Stir in ginger and garlic, curry and salt; cook 1 minute.

Stir in chicken broth, water, black pepper essential oil, lentils and tomato paste and bring to a boil. Reduce heat; simmer, covered for 25 minutes or until lentils are tender.

*See introduction page for delivery method.

Feisty Baked Chicken

1/4 cup fresh lemon juice

2 drops lime essential oil

3 tablespoons soy sauce

2 tablespoons honey

2 tablespoons chipotle chile in
adobo sauce

4 boneless, skinless chicken
breasts

In a large bowl, mix first 5 ingredients together. Add the chicken and coat with the mixture. Remove chicken from the mixture and place in a baking dish coated with a non-stick cooking spray. Bake at 400 degrees for 15 minutes.

Place remaining marinade in a blender and process until smooth. Place the marinade in a saucepan. Bring to a boil and cook for 3 minutes. Pour the marinade over the chicken; return to oven and bake an additional 20 minutes.

Baked Maple Chicken Breasts

1/4 cup extra virgin olive oil

3 cloves garlic, minced

1/4 cup fig balsamic vinegar

1 tablespoon pure maple syrup

1 drop lemon essential oil

4-5 boneless, skinless chicken
   breasts

1 teaspoon pepper

1 teaspoon salt

Preheat oven to 350 degrees. Combine olive oil, garlic, fig balsamic vinegar, lemon essential oil and syrup in a large bowl. Add chicken, and toss to coat; reserve marinade.

Place chicken in a baking dish sprayed with non-stick spray. Sprinkle with pepper and salt. Pour marinade over the chicken breasts. Bake at 350 degrees for 40 minutes.

Salmon with Creamy Dill Sauce

Dill Sauce:

1/3 cup sour cream

1/3 cup mayonnaise

1 tablespoon finely chopped
   green onion

1/8 cup cilantro

1 teaspoon parsley

1 drop lemon essential oil

1 spoon swirl dill essential oil*

1/4 teaspoon garlic salt

Dash of pepper

Remove the skin from 2-3 salmon filets. Set the oven rack about 6 inches from the top heat source. Preheat the oven to the broiler setting. Line a jelly roll pan with aluminum foil, and spray with nonstick spray. Place the salmon filets on the aluminum foil. Broil for approximately 9 minutes or until the fish flakes easily with a fork. Top with Dill Sauce.

*See introduction page for delivery method.

Tandorri Chicken

5 boneless, skinless chicken
  breasts

1 small onion

5 cloves garlic, minced

3 drops ginger essential oil

1 cup Greek yogurt

1 1/2 teaspoons cumin

1 teaspoon allspice

1 teaspoon ground cinnamon

1 teaspoon ground curry

1/2 teaspoon ground black
  pepper

1/2 teaspoon ground red
  pepper

Combine onion, garlic, ginger
essential oil, yogurt, cumin,
allspice, cinnamon, curry, black
pepper, and red pepper in a
food processor and blend until
smooth. Set half of the yogurt

mixture aside and store in the
refrigerator. Cut the chicken into bite
sized pieces and put in a large ziplock
bag.

Pour the remaining half of the mixture
over the chicken. Seal the ziplock bag
and mix well, to cover all of the
chicken. Place in the refrigerator and
chill overnight.

Add the chicken mixture to a skillet and
cook over medium high heat for
approximately 6-8 minutes, or until
there is no pink in the middle. Warm
the remaining half of the yogurt
mixture. Place cooked chicken over
steamed rice and top with yogurt
mixture.

Chicken Pesto Mozzarella

6-8 ounces linguine pasta

4 boneless, skinless chicken
  breasts

Salt and pepper

1 tablespoon olive oil

1, 14.5 ounce can diced
  tomatoes with basil, garlic
  and oregano

1/2 onion, chopped

1/2 cup pesto sauce*

1 small can sliced black olives

1/2 cup shredded mozzarella
  cheese

Cook pasta according to the package directions; drain. As pasta cooks, season the chicken with salt and pepper. In a skillet over medium-high heat, heat olive oil. Brown chicken on both sides.

In a small bowl, mix tomatoes, onion and olives together. Pour over chicken. Bring mixture to a boil; reduce heat to medium. Cover and cook approximately 8-10 minutes, or until chicken juice runs clear when cut in the middle.

Spread the pesto sauce over each chicken breast; sprinkle with cheese. Cover and continue cooking until the cheese melts. Serve over cooked pasta.

*If desired, substitute Greek Feta Pesto sauce. Recipe in the Edible Extras section.

Zesty Lemon Pasta

1 pound spaghetti

1 1/2 cup basil leaves

1 teaspoon thyme leaves

1 tablespoon oregano leaves

2 tablespoons olive oil

2 drops lemon essential oil

1 tablespoon lemon juice

2 tablespoons butter

1/2 teaspoon kosher salt

1/4 teaspoon black pepper

1/4 cup grated parmesan cheese

Bring a pot of water to a boil and cook pasta according to package directions. Blend the herbs, olive oil, lemon essential oil and lemon juice in a food processor.

When pasta is al dente, drain and toss with herb mixture, butter, salt, and black pepper. Garnish with parmesan cheese.

Mushroom Stuffed Chicken

1/4 cup breadcrumbs

1/4 cup green onions, chopped

1 cup mushrooms, sliced

1/2 teaspoon dried thyme

2 garlic cloves, minced

1/2 cup mozzarella cheese, shredded

1/2 teaspoon salt

1 spoon swirl black pepper essential oil*

4 boneless, skinless chicken breasts

1/4 cup flour

2 large eggs, lightly beaten

Preheat oven to 350 degrees. Heat a large non-stick skillet to medium-high heat.

Add onions and mushroom and sauté 10 minutes. Stir in the thyme and garlic.

Remove the mixture from the heat and allow to cool 10-15 minutes. Stir in the cheese, salt and pepper.

Sprinkle the chicken with salt and pepper. Place the flour in a shallow dish. Place the eggs in a separate shallow dish. Coat the chicken in the flour, dip in eggs and coat with breadcrumbs.

Cut a slit through the thickest portion of each chicken breast. Stuff each breast with 1/4 cup of mushroom mixture.

Place the chicken in a 9 x 13 inch baking dish, and bake at 350 degrees for 40 minutes or until chicken juice is clear when center of thickest part is cut.

*See introduction page for delivery method.

Jamaican Jerk Chicken

1 pound boneless, skinless
   chicken breast, cut into chunks

2 red bell peppers, cut into
   1 inch pieces

1 can cubed pineapples, drained

2 green onions, chopped

1 jalapeno, seeded and chopped

4 tablespoons olive oil

1 drop ginger essential oil

4 tablespoons white wine vinegar

2 tablespoons ground allspice

1 teaspoon dried thyme

1 teaspoon salt

Cut the chicken into bite-sized chunks and set aside. Add remaining ingredients in a blender and blend on high speed.

Place the chicken chunks into a large ziplock bag and pour marinade over the chicken, turning to coat. Place in the refrigerator for 30 minutes.

In a separate bowl, add another tablespoon of olive oil and red peppers and toss. Place the broiler rack close to the heat source and turn broiler on high.

On four metal skewers, alternately thread chicken, red pepper and pineapple chunks. Brush the kabobs with remaining marinade.

Cook a total of ten minutes, turning once, or until chicken is no longer pink inside.

Seafood Fettuccini Alfredo

8 ounces dry fettuccini

2 tablespoons butter

2 tablespoons garlic, minced

8 ounces small shrimp, peeled
  and deveined

8 ounces bay scallops

1/8 teaspoon salt

1/8 teaspoon pepper

1 spoon swirl nutmeg essential
  oil*

8 ounces heavy cream

1/2 cup parmesan cheese, grated

Boil the fettuccini to the al dente stage. Drain well. Heat a skillet to medium heat and sauté the garlic in butter, about 1 minute.

Add the scallops and sauté for 2 minutes. Turn the scallops over, toss in shrimp and cook both another 2 minutes.

Add the cream, salt, pepper, spoon swirl of nutmeg essential oil and parmesan cheese. Cook and stir until reduced to a light cream sauce. Pour the sauce over the fettuccini.

*See introduction page for delivery method.

Chickpea Chicken Curry with Jasmine Rice

3 boneless, skinless chicken
  breasts
1 cup jasmine rice, cooked
2 tablespoons olive oil
1 drop cinnamon essential oil
1 onion, chopped
2 cloves garlic, minced
1 teaspoon ginger powder
1 tablespoon curry powder
2 tomatoes, chopped
1 can chickpeas, drained and
  rinsed
3 tablespoons fresh cilantro,
  chopped

Cook rice according to package directions.

Cut chicken breast into bite size pieces. Heat oil and cinnamon essential oil in a large skillet over medium heat; add chicken, onion, garlic and ginger. Sauté 2 minutes or until onion is tender; stir in curry powder and tomatoes. Cook 6 minutes or until tomatoes are very tender and sauce is thickened.

Add chickpeas and 1 cup water. Cook 15 minutes or until thickened. Serve chicken mixture over cooked jasmine rice, and sprinkle with cilantro.

Sweet and Sour Quinoa Turkey Meatballs

1 pound lean ground turkey

2/3 cup cooked quinoa

3 garlic cloves, minced

1 egg

1/4 cup red onion, diced

1 drop black pepper essential oil

1/4 cup fresh parsley or cilantro, chopped

1/4 teaspoon dried basil

1/4 teaspoon dried oregano

Dash of salt

1, 20 ounce bottle of ketchup

1 jar grape jelly

Fresh chopped parsley (optional)

Preheat oven to 350 degrees. Thoroughly cover a baking sheet with parchment paper or cooking spray. In a large bowl add ground turkey, quinoa, red onion, garlic, parsley, basil, and oregano.

In a small bowl whisk together the egg, salt and black pepper essential oil. Add egg mixture to turkey mixture and mix well to combine. Roll into 1 inch balls and add to prepared baking sheet, spacing evenly. Bake for 30 minutes or until the meatballs are firm and cooked throughout.

While the meatballs are baking, heat the ketchup and grape jelly in a large saucepan and whisk together. Transfer the meatballs to the sauce and stir to coat them. Sprinkle some parsley on top (optional).

Spicy Curry Chicken

1 pound skinless, boneless
   chicken breasts

4 tablespoons olive oil

1 red pepper, finely chopped

1 small onion, finely chopped

1 drop black pepper essential oil

1 small can diced green chilies

2 tablespoons garlic, minced

1 drop ginger essential oil

2 tablespoons chili powder

1/4 teaspoon curry

1/4 teaspoon cumin

Cut chicken into bite size pieces and set aside. In a large skillet, heat the olive oil and black pepper essential oil in the pan over medium-high heat and sauté the red pepper and onion until the onion is golden brown. Add remaining ingredients to skillet and mix well.

Pour 2 cups of water into the mixture and stir well. Add the chicken pieces to the mixture and stir. Cover the skillet and let simmer about 15 minutes or until chicken is cooked thoroughly. Serve over cooked jasmine or brown rice.

Curry Dill Chicken

6 boneless, skinless chicken
  breasts
2 tablespoons flour
1/4 teaspoon salt
Dash of pepper
1 cup milk
1/4 cup mayonnaise
1 spoon swirl dill essential oil*
1/4 teaspoon curry powder
1 tablespoon olive oil

In a saucepan over medium heat, melt butter. Add the flour, salt and pepper and stir until smooth. Add milk and bring to a boil. Boil and stir for 2 minutes. Remove from the heat. Add mayonnaise, dill essential oil and curry; stir until smooth.

Spray a 9 x 13 baking dish with a non-stick cooking spray. Add the chicken breasts. Pour the sauce over the chicken. Bake at 350 degrees for 35 minutes or until the chicken juices run clear when cut in half.

*See introduction page for delivery method.

Spicy Asian Steak Stir Fry

2 tablespoons soy sauce

2 drops lime essential oil

1 spoon swirl ginger essential oil*

1 teaspoon curry powder

1/2 teaspoon red pepper flakes

1 1/2 teaspoons rice wine vinegar

1 teaspoon olive oil, divided

1 teaspoon sesame oil

1, 8 ounce can diced pineapple, drained

3 tablespoons minced fresh garlic

1 pound top sirloin steak, cut into strips

1 cup fresh red peppers, cut into bite size pieces

1 cup sugar snap peas

1 tablespoon vegetable oil

Combine first 10 ingredients in a small mixing bowl and mix well. Pour the marinade into large zip lock bag. Add strips of steak; seal the bag and coat steak with the marinade. Refrigerate marinated steak for 2 hours or overnight. Heat large nonstick skillet over medium-high heat. Add the vegetable oil. Add the red peppers and sugar snap peas. Cook and stir 2-4 minutes or until cooked to crisp tender. Remove from pan and set aside.

Remove beef from marinade; discard marinade. Stir fry for 2-3 minutes or until the outside surface of beef is no longer pink. Add the vegetables back into the skillet and toss together with the cooked beef. Cook vegetables until crisp tender. Serve over brown or jasmine rice (optional).

*See introduction page for delivery method.

Grilled Shrimp with Roasted Chile Rice

Rice:

2 tablespoons diced green chilies

1/2 cup fresh cilantro

1/4 cup fresh parsley

1 teaspoon lemon juice

1 drop lime essential oil

2 teaspoons olive oil

2 teaspoons white vinegar

1 teaspoon garlic, minced

Dash of salt and pepper

4 cups cooked jasmine rice

Shrimp:

1 pound raw large shrimp,
   peeled and deveined

1/2 teaspoon garlic, minced

2 tablespoon olive oil

Cook rice and set aside. Add green chilies, cilantro, parsley, lemon juice, lime essential oil, white vinegar, garlic and salt and pepper into a blender. Blend until smooth. Add the blender mixture into the rice and mix well.

Heat large nonstick skillet over medium-high heat. Add the shrimp, garlic and olive oil, a dash of salt and pepper and toss together in the skillet. Cook for 8-10 minutes, turning once during cooking time. Serve shrimp over rice.

Chicken Picadillo

1 pound boneless, skinless
   chicken breasts

2 teaspoons extra virgin olive oil

1/2 cup chopped onion

1 1/2 teaspoon ground cumin

1/2 teaspoon salt

1 drop cinnamon essential oil

2 garlic cloves, minced

1 cup salsa

1/3 cup golden raisins

1/3 cup slivered almonds

1/4 cup fresh cilantro, chopped

Place chicken in a food processor and pulse until ground.

Heat olive oil in a large nonstick skillet over medium-high heat. Add onions and cook for 4 minutes, stirring occasionally. Add chicken, cumin, salt, cinnamon essential oil, and garlic and cook for 3 minutes or until chicken is done, stirring frequently. Stir in the salsa and raisins. Cover, reduce heat and simmer for 5-7 minutes or until heated thoroughly.

Stir in almonds and cilantro. Serve with rice and black beans.

Herb and Lemon Halibut

3-4 Halibut steaks

Marinade:

1/4 cup extra virgin olive oil

2 drops lemon essential oil

1 spoon swirl rosemary
  essential oil*

1 tablespoon fresh dill, minced

Herb butter:

1/4 cup butter

2 drops lemon essential oil

1 tablespoon fresh parsley,
  minced

1/8 teaspoon salt

1/8 teaspoon cayenne

In a mixing bowl, whisk the marinade ingredients together. Place the halibut steaks into the marinade and coat both sides. Cover and refrigerate for 30 minutes.

Melt the butter in a small mixing bowl. Add the remaining ingredients to the melted butter, stir well, and chill in the refrigerator for 30 minutes.

Preheat oven to 450 degrees. Spray a shallow baking dish with a non-stick cooking spray. Add the marinated halibut steaks to the baking dish. Bake for 12-15 minutes, or until the halibut is flaky.

*See introduction page for delivery method.

Orzo Salad with Lemon Chickpeas and Dill

1 cup uncooked orzo

2 boneless, skinless chicken breasts, cooked and chopped (optional)

1/4 cup green onions, chopped

1 cup crumbled feta cheese

1 teaspoon dill (dried)

1, 19 ounce can chickpeas, drained

3 tablespoon kalamata olives, pitted and chopped

2 drops lemon essential oil

1 1/2 tablespoons extra-virgin olive oil

2 tablespoons water

1/2 teaspoon salt

1/2 teaspoon fresh garlic, chopped

Cook orzo pasta according to the package directions. Rinse with cold water and drain.

Boil chicken breasts for approximately 20 minutes, or until cooked thoroughly.

Combine pasta, cooked chicken, onions, cheese, dill, chickpeas and kalamata olives in a large bowl. Combine lemon essential oil, olive oil, water, salt and garlic in a small bowl. Add to pasta mixture and stir.

Grilled Salmon with Summer Fruit Chutney

2 salmon fillets

1 tablespoon olive oil

2 tablespoons curry powder

2 drops lemon essential oil

1 nectarine, pitted and diced

1 plum, pitted and diced

1/3 cup blueberries

1 tablespoons green onion, chopped

1/8 teaspoon cayenne pepper

2 tablespoons fresh cilantro, chopped

Dash of salt and pepper

Mix the olive oil, curry powder and 1 drop of lemon essential oil together. Brush on top of the salmon fillets, and bake at 350 degrees for 15-20 minutes.

Mix 1 drop of lemon essential oil and the remaining ingredients together. Spoon over the cooked salmon.

Ginger Stir Fry

Couscous

2 tablespoons peanut oil*

7 green onions, chopped

7 baby carrots, julienne

2 garlic cloves, chopped

3/4 cup raw cashews*

2 cups snow peas

1/2 red pepper, julienne

3/4 cup bean sprouts

2 drops ginger essential oil

1-2 drops black pepper essential
  oil

1-2 limes, juiced

Cook couscous according to
package directions.

In wok or deep fry pan, heat peanut oil on medium heat. Add green onions, carrots, and garlic. Cook for 2-3 minutes. Add cashews, snow peas, and red pepper. Cook for another 2-3 minutes. If vegetables and cashews start to stick, drizzle with more peanut oil. Add bean sprouts, ginger essential oil, black pepper essential oil and toss. Cook for another 1-2 minutes. Serve over couscous or brown rice and squeeze fresh limes on top.

*Peanut oil may be exchanged for extra virgin olive oil; cashews can be removed for those with nut allergies.

Black Pepper BBQ Burgers

1 pound extra lean ground beef

1/2 cup grated cheese (of your choice)

1/4 cup BBQ sauce

1 spoon swirl black pepper essential oil*

Salt to taste

1/4 teaspoon onion powder

A few dashes Tabasco® sauce

Mix all of the ingredients into the ground beef. Make into hamburger patties. Grill on the BBQ for 15-20 minutes, or to your liking. Serve with buns or protein style (hamburger wrapped in red leaf lettuce).

*See introduction page for delivery method.

Lemon Greek Yogurt Chicken

1 cup plain, Greek yogurt

4 drops lemon essential oil

2 tablespoons fresh oregano, finely chopped

2 tablespoons fresh parsley, finely chopped

1 clove glove, chopped

1/4 teaspoon salt

1/8 teaspoon pepper

4 boneless, skinless chicken breasts

Combine the yogurt, lemon essential oil, oregano, parsley, garlic, salt and pepper. Place the chicken into a baking dish and spread the yogurt mixture over the chicken. Bake at 375 degrees for 30 minutes.

Creamy Chipotle Lime Chicken

1 cup mayonnaise

2 drops lime essential oil

2 tablespoons fresh cilantro, chopped

2 cloves garlic, finely chopped

1 chipotle pepper in adobo sauce, finely chopped

2 pounds boneless, skinless chicken breasts

Mix the first five ingredients together. Cut the chicken breasts into bite sized pieces. Place the chicken in a baking dish, pour the mixture over the chicken, and cook at 350 degrees for 30 minutes. Serve over brown rice.

Chipotle Turkey Burgers

1 pound ground turkey

1/2 cup onion, finely chopped

2 tablespoons fresh cilantro,
   finely chopped

1 chipotle chile in adobo sauce,
   finely chopped

1 teaspoon garlic powder

1 teaspoon onion powder

1 teaspoon salt

1 drop black pepper essential oil

4 slices pepperjack cheese

Mix all ingredients into the ground turkey and make into patties. Grill on the BBQ for 15-20 minutes or to your liking.

Remove from the grill, and place a slice of cheese on top of the turkey burger.

Top with Spicy Southwestern Slaw* and serve with bun or protein style (hamburger wrapped in red leaf lettuce).

* Spicy Southwestern Slaw can be found in the Edible Extras section.

Italian Chicken Parmesan

1 cup of breadcrumbs

1 tablespoon Italian Seasoning

1/4 cup of parmesan cheese

Mix together and set aside.

1 jar organic marinara sauce

1 spoon swirl oregano oil*

1 drop basil essential oil

Dash red pepper flakes

4 skinless, boneless, chicken
  breasts

1 spoon swirl black pepper
  essential oil*

1 large egg, lightly beaten

1 teaspoon water

1/2 cup fresh parsley leaves,
  chopped

2 teaspoons garlic powder

Fresh mozzarella, thinly sliced

Preheat the oven to 350 degrees. Combine the marinara sauce, oregano and basil essential oil and dash of red pepper flakes in a saucepan. Let simmer for 15 minutes.

In a large mixing bowl, combine the eggs, water and black pepper essential oil, beat until frothy. Put the breadcrumbs on a plate, dip the chicken breast in the egg mixture and coat with breadcrumbs.

Place the chicken breast in a baking dish and pour the marinara sauce over the breaded chicken. Add a slice of mozzarella cheese on top of each piece of chicken. Bake for 35 minutes, or until chicken is no longer pink inside.

*See introduction page for delivery method.

Lemon Pepper Steak

1/3 cup red Zinfandel

1/3 cup Worcestershire sauce

1 teaspoon lemon pepper

1/2 teaspoon onion powder

1 tablespoon parsley

1 teaspoon garlic salt

1 drop black pepper essential oil

1 drop lemon essential oil

Combine all ingredients in a mixing bowl, and pour over steaks. Marinate for one hour. Grill or cook steaks as desired.

Chicken Fettuccini Alfredo

1 package dry fettuccini noodles

2 tablespoons butter

2 tablespoons chopped garlic

3 pre-cooked chicken breasts, chopped

Dash of salt

1 spoon swirl black pepper essential oil*

1 spoon swirl nutmeg essential oil*

8 ounces heavy cream

1/2 cup grated parmesan cheese

1 teaspoon chopped fresh parsley (optional)

Boil the fettuccini according to the package directions. Drain well. Sauté the garlic in butter. Add cream, salt, parmesan cheese, black pepper and nutmeg essential oils; whisk together.

Add the cooked chicken breasts. Cook and stir until reduced to a light cream sauce. Add to the cooked fettuccine the chicken mixture, and toss well. Sprinkle with chopped parsley.

*See introduction page for delivery method.

Edible Extras

Greek Feta Pesto

1/4 cup extra virgin olive oil

2 cups fresh basil leaves

1 small can sliced black olives, drained

1/2 cup feta cheese, crumbled

4 cloves garlic, peeled

Dash of salt

1 spoon swirl black pepper essential oil*

Combine all ingredients in a food processor and process until nearly smooth. Serve with pita bread, or mix with pasta.

*See introduction page for delivery method.

Spicy Southwestern Slaw

1 1/2 cups mayonnaise

1/2 cup cider vinegar

1/8 teaspoon stevia (powdered)

1 tablespoon Tabasco

2 teaspoons salt

1 drop black pepper essential oil

1/2 head green cabbage, thinly
  sliced

1/2 head red cabbage, thinly
  sliced

1/2 cup green onion, finely
  chopped

1 small red bell pepper, cut into
  thin strips

Mix all ingredients in a bowl. Serve as a side dish or on top of the chipotle turkey burger.*

*Recipe for the chipotle turkey burger found in the Main Dishes section.

Chipotle Mayonnaise

1/2 cup mayonnaise

2 chipotle chilies in adobo sauce

1 teaspoon adobo sauce

1 spoon swirl lime essential oil*

1 clove garlic, chopped

Blend together in a food processor or blender.

*See introduction page for delivery method.

Berry Granola

2 cups whole rolled oats*

1/2 cup raw nuts, chopped

1/4 cup raw pumpkin seeds

1/2 cup unsweetened dried
berries, chopped

2-3 tablespoons maple syrup or
raw honey (or a combo of
both)

2 tablespoons virgin coconut oil

1/2 teaspoon vanilla extract

1 large pinch fine sea salt

1 drop cinnamon essential oil

Preheat the oven to 300 degrees. Combine all ingredients in a mixing bowl, use your hands to mix well and toss to coat. Spread the mixture in a thin layer on a baking sheet and bake for 10 minutes, until very lightly toasted. Cool before serving or storing. This granola can be kept in an airtight container in a cool, dry place for up to 2 weeks.

*Can substitute rolled oats with gluten free rolled oats

Lemon Caper Tartar Sauce

1/2 cup mayonnaise

2 tablespoons dill pickle, finely
  chopped

1 drop lemon essential oil

1 teaspoon dill

1 teaspoon white wine vinegar

1/2 teaspoon dry mustard

1 tablespoon capers

Dash of ground pepper

Mix all of the ingredients together and
serve with fish.

Amy's Basil Dressing

2 tablespoons red wine vinegar

2 tablespoons balsamic vinegar

3 tablespoons fresh basil,
   coarsely chopped

1 drop basil essential oil

1 tablespoon sugar or dash of
   powdered stevia

2 cloves garlic, chopped

1/2 cup extra virgin olive oil

1/2 teaspoon salt

Dash of fresh ground pepper

Place all of ingredients in a food processor. Mix in short bursts until blended.

Cilantro Orange Dressing

1/2 cup mayonnaise

1/4 cup orange juice

1 tablespoon honey

1 tablespoon white wine vinegar

1 drop orange essential oil

1 spoon swirl ginger essential
   oil*

2 tablespoons fresh cilantro

1/2 teaspoon vanilla extract

Combine all ingredients in a blender or
food processor and mix thoroughly.

*See introduction page for delivery
method.

Garlic Parmesan Chickpeas

2 cups canned chickpeas, drained

1 tablespoon olive oil

1 clove garlic, minced

1/4 cup parmesan cheese,
   shredded

Dash of sea salt

1 spoon swirl black pepper
   essential oil*

Preheat oven to 375 degrees. Rinse chickpeas and pat dry. Spread onto a baking sheet and bake for 30 minutes, or until crunchy.

In a mixing bowl combine olive oil, garlic, parmesan cheese, salt and black pepper essential oil and combine. (Do this as soon as the chickpeas come out of the oven.) Toss the roasted chickpeas with the olive oil mixture. Serve warm.

*See introduction page for delivery method.

Vegetables

Lemon Mint Peas

2 cups frozen green peas

1 tablespoon butter

1 spoon swirl peppermint
  essential oil*

1 drop lemon essential oil

1/4 teaspoon ground pepper

1/8 teaspoon salt

Combine the frozen green peas with 2 tablespoons of water in a bowl. Cover and microwave on high for three minutes, stirring at two minutes. Drain the water off the peas.

Combine the remaining ingredients in a mixing bowl and stir the peas into the mixture. Serve hot.

*See introduction page for delivery method.

Roasted Red Pepper Asiago Broccoli

1 1/2 pounds broccoli

3 tablespoons olive oil

1 drop black pepper
   essential oil

1/8 teaspoon crushed red
   pepper flakes

1 1/4 cup grated asiago cheese

Preheat oven to 450 degrees. Cut the crowns of the broccoli from the stalk. Combine the olive oil, black pepper essential oil and red pepper flakes into a large mixing bowl. Add the broccoli crowns and coat with the olive oil mixture.

Transfer the broccoli to a casserole dish. Roast until crisp-tender and the tips begin to brown (approximately 25 minutes). Sprinkle with asiago cheese and return to the oven on the broil setting. Cook until the cheese turns a golden brown.

Black Pepper Kale

1 bunch kale, sliced

1/3 cup water

1/4 cup olive oil

1 teaspoon garlic, chopped

1 drop black pepper essential oil

Dash of salt

Sliced almonds or pine nuts

Combine all ingredients together in a skillet and cover on low to medium heat for 10 minutes, stirring occasionally. Take the lid off and continue cooking until the water evaporates. Transfer to plate and sprinkle sliced nuts on top.

Roasted Sweet Potatoes with Chile Yogurt

4 pounds medium sweet
potatoes

2 tablespoons extra virgin olive
oil, plus more for drizzling

2 1/2 cups plain Greek yogurt

1 Serrano chile, finely grated

2 drops lemon essential oil

2 teaspoons fresh lime juice

2 tablespoons toasted sesame
seeds

1 1/2 cups mint leaves, torn

Sea salt

Preheat oven to 400 degrees.
Toss sweet potatoes with 2
tablespoons olive oil on a
parchment-lined rimmed baking
sheet.

Roast, turning halfway through, until
tender, 50–60 minutes. Remove from
oven; increase oven temperature to
450 degrees. Let sweet potatoes cool
slightly, then tear into large pieces
(including skin). Spread out on the
same baking sheet and roast until
browned and crisp around the edges,
20–25 minutes.

Combine yogurt, chile, lemon essential
oil, and lime juice in a medium bowl.
Coarsely crush sesame seeds on a
cutting board.

Spread chile yogurt on a platter; top
with sweet potatoes. Scatter mint,
sesame seeds, and sea salt over the
sweet potatoes. Drizzle with olive oil.

Ginger Green Beans

1 1/2 pounds fresh green beans, trimmed and cut in half (about 5 cups)

5 tablespoons unsalted butter

2 drops ginger essential oil

1/2 cup chicken broth

1/2 teaspoon salt

1/4 teaspoon freshly ground black pepper

1 cup salted cashews, coarsely chopped

In a large pot of boiling water, cook the green beans until crisp-tender, about four minutes. Drain the green beans and run them under cold running water. Drain well and pat dry with a paper towel. In a skillet, melt the butter over medium heat. Stir in the ginger essential oil.

Add the green beans and chicken broth, and sauté until the liquid is completely evaporated (about 6 minutes). Add cashews and sauté for one minute. Stir in the salt and pepper. Transfer to a serving dish and serve immediately.

Grilled Asparagus with Garlic and Parmesan Cheese

1 bunch asparagus

2 garlic cloves, peeled and
  minced

3 tablespoons grated parmesan
  cheese

3 tablespoons olive oil

1 spoon swirl black pepper
  essential oil*

Sea salt to taste

Wash the asparagus, cut the ends off and place them in a large bowl. Preheat the grill.

In a separate bowl, combine the remaining ingredients. Pour over the asparagus and toss until well-coated.

Lay the asparagus spears on the grill crosswise over a medium flame. Grill for about 5 minutes, turning often to prevent them from burning. Grilling times will depend on the size of the asparagus.

*See introduction page for delivery method.

Zucchini Pepper Pancakes

5 medium zucchini

3/4 teaspoon Celtic Sea Salt

4 eggs

1 clove garlic, minced

3/4 cup flour or gluten-free flour

1/2 cup grated parmesan cheese

1 tablespoon green onion, finely
    chopped

1 spoon swirl black pepper
    essential oil*

Extra virgin olive oil

Trim and grate the zucchini. Squeeze the excess liquid from the zucchini and pat with a paper towel. It is important to remove as much excess liquid as possible.

Beat the eggs and garlic together. Stir in the flour, cheese, onions and black pepper essential oil. Add the shredded zucchini to the mix and combine well.

Pour a small amount of extra virgin olive oil in a griddle or skillet until it thinly coats the bottom of the skillet. Cook over medium heat 3 minutes on each side, or until the pancake is golden brown. Serve with sour cream (optional).

*See introduction page for delivery method.

Glazed Yams

2 tablespoons butter

1 large can cooked yams,

  drained

1/8 cup brown sugar

1/4 cup orange juice

Dash of salt

1 drop lemon essential oil

1 drop cinnamon essential oil

Add all ingredients (except the yams) into a sauce pan and stir together. Add yams and coat with glaze. Cook on low heat for approximately 10 minutes, or until hot.

Cheesy Basil Zucchini Casserole

6 to 8 medium zucchini

1 medium onion, chopped

2 tablespoons butter

12 ounce can tomato paste

8 ounce can tomato sauce

1/4 teaspoon salt

1/4 teaspoon pepper

1/2 teaspoon garlic powder

1/2 teaspoon Italian seasoning

1 drop basil essential oil

1/2 teaspoon oregano

1 3/4 cups grated cheddar
   cheese

1/2 cup grated mozzarella
   cheese

Wash the zucchini and slice into 1/2 inch pieces. Steam for 5 minutes (do not overcook); set aside.

Sauté the onion in the butter until crisp tender; set aside. Add tomato paste, tomato sauce, basil essential oil and seasonings together and mix well.

Grease a 9 x 13 inch baking dish. Layer half the zucchini, half the onion, half the sauce and half the cheddar cheese in the casserole dish. Repeat. Top with mozzarella cheese. Bake, uncovered, at 350 degrees for 30 minutes, or until the vegetables are heated through and the cheese bubbles.

Slow Cooker

Mediterranean Beef Stew

2 pounds chuck steak, cut into
   bite-sized pieces

1 portabello mushroom, sliced

1 onion, chopped

1 cup beef stock

1 cup tomato sauce

1/4 cup balsamic vinegar

1/2 cup kalamata olives, halved

1/2 cup marinated artichoke
   hearts, chopped

2 garlic cloves, chopped

1 drop rosemary essential oil

1 drop black pepper essential oil

2 tablespoons finely chopped fresh
   parsley

1 tablespoons capers

Dash salt

Place all ingredients together in a slow cooker. Cook on low for 8 hours.

Spanish Chicken with Spicy Lemon Rice

2 tablespoons paprika

1 tablespoon garlic powder

Salt and pepper

6 boneless, skinless chicken
breasts

14 ounce can diced tomatoes
with green onion and bell
pepper

1 red bell pepper, diced into 2
inch pieces

1/2 onion, diced

2 tablespoons tomato paste

2 cups chicken broth

1 cup rice

1/2 teaspoon red pepper flakes

2 drops lemon essential oil

1 cup pitted garlic stuffed
olives, chopped

In a large ziplock bag, mix together paprika, garlic powder, a dash of salt and pepper. Add the chicken and toss to coat. Place in the bottom of a slow cooker.

In a mixing bowl add the tomato paste and chicken broth, and whisk together. Add the can of tomatoes, red bell pepper, onion and chopped garlic stuffed olives and mix well with the tomato paste mixture. Pour over the chicken. Cook on low for 4 hours.

In a medium pot, combine 2 cups water, rice, red pepper flakes, lemon essential oil and a dash of salt. Bring to a boil and cook until the rice is tender and has absorbed all of the liquid.

Serve the chicken over the rice.

Five Spice Pork Ribs

5 tablespoons soy sauce

1 tablespoons tomato paste

1 tablespoon Chinese Five Spice
   powder

2 teaspoons balsamic vinegar

2 drops ginger essential oil

2 teaspoons olive oil

1 teaspoon rice vinegar

3 garlic cloves, chopped

1 pound pork ribs, cut into
   individual pieces

Combine soy sauce, tomato paste, five spice, sugar, ginger essential oil, olive oil, vinegar and garlic in a bowl. Spread mixture evenly over ribs and transfer to a slow cooker. Cook on low heat for 6 hours or until tender.

Italian Chicken

3 boneless, skinless chicken
  breasts, cut in half

45 ounce canned Italian style
  tomatoes

16 ounces chickpeas

1/2 onion, diced

4 cloves garlic, chopped

1 cup pitted kalamata olives

2 tablespoons capers

2 cups chicken broth

1 teaspoon ground oregano

1 drop black pepper essential
  oil

Dash of salt

Feta cheese

Brown rice or mashed potatoes

Mix all ingredients together in a slow cooker (minus the feta cheese and brown rice/potatoes), and cook on low heat for 6-8 hours. Serve over brown rice or mashed potatoes. Sprinkle with feta cheese.

Black Bean Soup with Bacon

2, 15 ounce cans of black beans

4 strips thick cut bacon, cut
 into bite sized pieces

1 red pepper, chopped finely

1/2 onion, chopped finely

4 cloves garlic, chopped

1 1/2 teaspoons ground cumin

1 teaspoon ground oregano

1 chipotle in adobo, finely
 chopped

1 drop lime essential oil

3 tablespoons diced jalapenos

5 cups chicken broth

1 teaspoon brown sugar

1 tablespoon dry sherry

(optional)

Combine all ingredients into a slow cooker and cook for 6-8 hours on the low setting. Serve warm and top with sour cream.

Italian Pepperoncini Beef

4 pounds lean beef roast

1 jar (16 ounce) pepperoncini
  peppers

1 tablespoon garlic, minced

1 tablespoon ground oregano

1 drop basil essential oil

1 tablespoon Italian seasoning

1/4 cup red wine (optional)

Place the beef roast in the slow cooker. Drain the juice from the pepperoncini peppers into a small bowl. Add the drop of basil essential oil and the garlic to the juice and mix together. Add the pepperoncini and mix together. Pour over the beef.

Pour the red wine around the bottom of the roast.

Sprinkle the oregano and Italian seasoning over the top of the roast. Cover and cook on low 6-8 hours.

Beef and Cinnamon Sweet Potato Stew

1 1/2 pounds lean stew beef,
   cut into 1-inch cubes

1/2 teaspoon salt

1/4 teaspoon pepper

3 cups peeled sweet potatoes,
   cut into 1-inch cubes

2-3 garlic cloves, finely minced

Dash ground allspice

1 drop cinnamon essential oil

1/2 onion, cut into chunks

1 can (28 ounce) diced
   tomatoes, undrained

10 dried apricots, cut in half

Fresh parsley, chopped

Combine all ingredients (except parsley) into a slow cooker. Cover and cook on low for 6-8 hours, or until beef is tender. Top with fresh parsley.

Chicken Cacciatore

4 skinless, boneless chicken
  breasts

1/2 onion, peeled and chopped

2 carrots, peeled and chopped

2 cups sliced mushrooms

2-3 cloves garlic, minced

1 can (14 ounces) diced
  tomatoes

1 can (8 ounces) tomato paste

1 drop rosemary essential oil

1 tablespoon dried basil

1 cup chicken broth

Salt and pepper to taste

Polenta (optional)

Place chicken breasts in the slow cooker. Mix together the remaining ingredients. Cook for 6-8 hours on low. Serve over polenta.

Lime Cilantro Chicken Tacos

3 pounds boneless, skinless
  chicken breasts

1, 16 ounce jar salsa

2 tablespoon taco seasoning

3 drops lime essential oil

3 tablespoons fresh cilantro,
  chopped

1/2 cup chicken broth

2 cloves fresh garlic, chopped

Cut up the chicken into bite sized pieces and set aside. Add remaining ingredients into a slow cooker and mix together. Add the chicken and mix together with combined ingredients. Cook on low for 6-8 hours. Remove from the slow cooker, and shred the chicken with a spoon. Serve, using a slotted spoon on a corn tortilla with any of your favorite taco toppings.

Holiday Ham

1 (6 pound) bone-in country ham

3 cups apple cider

2 drops cinnamon essential oil

1 drop nutmeg essential oil

1 spoon swirl ginger essential oil*

2 drops clove essential oil

2 drops orange essential oil

3/4 cup brown sugar

1 cup maple syrup

Place the ham, fat side down, into the slow cooker.

Mix the cinnamon, nutmeg, ginger, clove and orange essential oils into the apple cider. Pour the apple cider mix over the ham, leaving approximately 2 inches of the ham above the surface. Pack the brown sugar on top of the ham. Pour the maple syrup over the ham. Cook on low for 8-10 hours.

*See introduction page for delivery method.

Side Dishes

Country Baked Beans

1 pound hamburger

3/4 pound bacon, cut up

1 cup chopped onion

2 cans pork and beans

1, 15 ounce can kidney beans

1, 15 ounce can pinto beans

1 cup ketchup

1/4 cup brown sugar

1 tablespoon liquid smoke

3 tablespoons white vinegar

2 drops black pepper essential oil

1 teaspoon salt

Brown the hamburger and drain the fat. Add the hamburger and all other ingredients to a crock-pot. Stir well; cover and cook on low for 4 to 6 hours.

Tangerine Honey Salad Dressing

2 tablespoons white wine
  vinegar

1/4 cup extra virgin olive oil

1 teaspoon honey

Dash of salt

Dash of pepper

Dash of cayenne pepper

2 drops tangerine essential oil

In a small bowl, whisk all ingredients together. Enjoy over your favorite tossed salad.

Sultana, Apple and Cinnamon Couscous

2 cups couscous

2/3 cup sultana

1/2 cup orange juice

1 drop cinnamon essential oil

1 apple, core removed, coarsely
  grated

8 ounces plain, Greek yogurt

1/2 teaspoon honey

1/4 cup toasted sliced almonds

Cook couscous according to package instructions. In a mixing bowl, whisk the orange juice and cinnamon essential oil together. Add the apple, Greek yogurt and honey and mix well. Add the cooked couscous to the mixture. Serve in a bowl, and top with toasted almonds.

Quinoa Greek Salad

1 cup quinoa

1 cucumber, peeled, seeded and
  diced

1 tomato, diced

2 stalks green onion, diced

1/4 cup feta cheese, crumbled

1/4 cup kalamata olives, sliced

3 tablespoons olive oil

3-5 drops lemon essential oil

Dash of salt and pepper

1 clove garlic, minced

1/8 cup dried cranberries

1/8 cup dates, chopped finely

Prepare the quinoa according to the package instructions. In a large mixing bowl, combine remaining ingredients and mix well. Add cooked quinoa and chill in the refrigerator. Serve cold.

Cheesy Baked Potatoes

1, 2 pound bags of frozen hash
   browns (cubed)

1 teaspoon salt

1 spoon swirl black pepper*

1/4 teaspoon white pepper

1/2 cup butter

1/2 medium onion, chopped

1 can cream of chicken soup

2 cups sour cream

2 1/2 cups grated cheddar
cheese

Sauté the onions and butter in a large skillet for about 10 minutes. In a large bowl, add the onion mixture together with the remaining ingredients and transfer to a 9 x 13 baking dish. Bake at 350 degrees for one hour.

*See introduction page for delivery method.

Curried Barley with Dates and Almonds

1 1/2 teaspoons olive oil

1 cup green onion, chopped

2 cloves garlic, minced

1 spoon swirl black pepper essential oil*

1 teaspoon curry powder

1 1/2 cups cooked pearl barley

2 tablespoons dates, chopped

2 tablespoons fresh parsley, chopped

2 tablespoons slivered almonds

1/4 teaspoon salt

Heat the olive oil and black pepper essential oil in a medium skillet over medium heat. Add green onion, garlic, and curry powder and sauté for two minutes.

Add the cooked barley, dates, parsley, slivered almonds, salt and pepper and mix together. Serve immediately.

*See introduction page for delivery method.

Parmesan Thyme Golden Potatoes

1 1/2 pound unpeeled Yukon
golden potatoes, cut into
1-inch chunks

2 tablespoons olive oil

1 teaspoon salt

1/4 teaspoon black pepper

1/2 cup grated parmesan cheese

1/4 teaspoon dried thyme leaves

1 spoon swirl rosemary
essential oil*

1/4 cup feta cheese

Preheat an oven to 400 degrees. Place the potatoes into a mixing bowl and coat with olive oil. Sprinkle with salt, pepper, parmesan cheese, and thyme. Toss evenly to coat and transfer to a 9" x 13" baking dish.

Bake for 1 hour. Remove from the oven and sprinkle with feta cheese.

*See introduction page for delivery method.

Cinnamon Baked Pumpkin

1/4 cup packed brown sugar

1 drop cinnamon essential oil

1/2 teaspoon salt

3 pounds baking pumpkin or
   winter squash (butternut or
   acorn), peeled, seeded

2 tablespoons butter, melted

Preheat oven to 325 degrees. Line a 3-quart rectangular baking dish with foil. In a small bowl, stir together brown sugar and salt; set aside. In another small bowl mix together melted butter and cinnamon essential oil.

Place the pumpkin into a prepared 3-quart baking dish. Brush pumpkin with butter mixture. Sprinkle brown sugar mixture evenly over pumpkin.

Bake covered with foil for 40 minutes. Uncover and stir pumpkin. Bake uncovered about 15 minutes more or until pumpkin is tender.

Italian Rosemary Marinade

1/2 cup extra virgin olive oil

1/4 cup fresh lemon juice

2 cloves garlic, minced

1 drop rosemary essential oil

2 drops lemon essential oil

1 teaspoon Italian seasoning

In a small bowl, combine all ingredients, mixing well. This tangy, herbed marinade is good for chicken and fish.

Peach Salsa

4 medium peaches, peeled and
pitted

1 large tomato, cut into wedges
and seeded

1/2 sweet onion, cut into
wedges

1/2 cup fresh cilantro leaves

2 garlic cloves, peeled and
crushed

2, 4 ounce cans chopped
green chilies

4 teaspoons cider vinegar

1 teaspoon lime juice

1/4 teaspoon pepper

Tortilla chips

In a food processor, combine the first five ingredients; cover and pulse until coarsely chopped. Add the chilies, vinegar, lime juice and pepper; cover and pulse until blended. Transfer to a serving bowl; chill until serving. Serve with chips.

Creamy Cheesy Basil Polenta

4 cups water

Salt to taste

1 cup yellow cornmeal

4 tablespoons butter

3 ounces cream cheese

1/2 cup fresh grated parmesan
  cheese

1/4 cup grated romano cheese

1 spoon swirl basil essential oil*

Heat water lightly seasoned with salt to a boil over high heat. Melt the butter in the water and quickly whisk in the cornmeal.

Lower the heat to a low simmer, and allow the polenta to cook, stirring occasionally, for 30 minutes.

Finish by stirring in the cream cheese, parmesan and romano cheese, basil essential oil and salt to taste.

*See introduction page for delivery method.

Basil Herb Brown Rice

2 teaspoons butter

1 garlic clove, minced

1 cup brown rice

1 cup water

1/4 teaspoon salt

1 spoon swirl basil essential oil*

1 teaspoon Italian seasoning

1/4 cup parmesan cheese

Melt the butter in a saucepan over medium heat. Add garlic and sauté for 1-2 minutes. Add water, basil essential oil and salt and bring to a boil. Stir in brown rice. Reduce heat, cover, and simmer for 20 minutes or until liquid is absorbed. Stir in the Italian seasoning and parmesan cheese.

*See introduction page for delivery method.

Spiced Cherry Sauce

3/4 cup sugar

Dash of salt

3 tablespoons cornstarch

1/2 teaspoon ground cloves

3/4 cup orange juice

1 drop lemon essential oil

1 spoon swirl cinnamon
   essential oil*

2 cups can pitted red tart
   cherries (water packed)

1 cinnamon stick

1/2 teaspoon red food color
   (optional)

Combine sugar, salt, cornstarch and cloves and whisk together. Stir in orange juice, lemon essential oil, and cinnamon essential oil. Add undrained cherries, cinnamon stick and food coloring. Mix well. Cook stirring constantly over medium heat until mixture thickens and comes to a boil. Boil two minutes. Remove cinnamon stick. Serve warm with ham.

*See introduction page for delivery method.

Herbed Sautéd Mushrooms

2 1/2 cups sliced mushrooms

1 drop dill essential oil

1/4 cup butter, melted

1 large onion, thinly sliced

2 tablespoons finely chopped
   fresh parsley

1 teaspoon garlic clove, minced

Dash of salt and pepper

Melt butter in skillet. Add one drop of dill essential oil and whisk into melted butter. Add mushrooms, and onions. Sauté for three minutes. Add remaining ingredients. Mix well, cover skillet and simmer for seven minutes. Keeping flame low, cook until liquid is absorbed, stirring frequently. Mushrooms should be medium dark brown when done.

Desserts

Peppermint Bark

2 Ghirardelli milk chocolate baking bars

3 Ghirardelli semi-sweet chocolate baking bars

5 Ghirardelli white chocolate baking bars

1 spoon swirl of peppermint essential oil*

20 peppermint candy canes

Unwrap the candy canes and place them in a food processor. Pulse on/off several times for 5-10 seconds each, until the canes have been crushed into small pieces. If you don't have a food processor, use a rolling pin to roll/smash the candy canes in a ziplock bag, until they are the size you desire.

Prepare a cookie sheet by covering it with wax or parchment paper.

Break the dark chocolate and milk chocolate bars into small pieces and place in a saucepan. Stir until melted over low heat. Add a spoon swirl of peppermint essential oil to the chocolate mixture. Pour the chocolate onto the prepared cookie sheet. Use a spatula to spread it to an even thickness. Place the tray in the refrigerator to firm up for approximately 30 minutes.

Break the white chocolate bars into small pieces and place in a saucepan. Stir until melted over low heat. Stir in most of the candy cane bits, reserving about a quarter of the mixture to put on top.

Remove the tray of dark chocolate from the refrigerator and spread the white chocolate in an even layer over the dark chocolate.

Sprinkle the remaining candy cane pieces over the entire surface evenly. Press down slightly to ensure they stick. Place the tray back in the refrigerator for approximately 30 minutes. Once the peppermint bark is completely set, break into small, uneven pieces by hand.

*See introduction page for delivery method.

Pumpkin Pie
with Cinnamon Whipped Cream

Pumpkin Pie:

1 unbaked 9-inch deep dish
  pie shell

3/4 cup sugar

1/2 teaspoon salt

1 teaspoon ground cinnamon

1/2 teaspoon ground ginger

1/4 teaspoon ground cloves

2 eggs

1, 15 ounce can pure pumpkin

1 1/4 cup half and half

Combine sugar, salt, cinnamon, ginger and cloves in a small bowl. Beat the eggs in a large bowl. Stir in the pumpkin and add to spice mixture. Stir in half and half.

Pour into uncooked pie shell. Bake at 350 degrees for 55 minutes, or until knife inserted near center comes out clean. Serve immediately or chill.

Cinnamon Whipped Cream:

1 pint heavy whipping cream

1 tablespoon sugar

1/4 teaspoon vanilla

1 spoon swirl cinnamon essential oil*

In a large bowl, combine ingredients together and mix with a blender on high speed until stiff peaks are just about to form.

*See introduction page for delivery method.

Cinnamon Baked Apples

2 Gala apples

4 tablespoons butter, divided

1/4 cup organic brown sugar

2 drops lemon essential oil

1 drop cinnamon essential oil

1/4 teaspoon vanilla

Cut the top and bottom off of the apple, and core the apple Butter the top and the sides of the apple with 2 tablespoons butter.

Put the brown sugar in a bowl and roll the top and buttered sides of the apple in brown sugar Place in a baking dish, bottom side down.

Combine the remaining butter, lemon essential oil, cinnamon essential oil and vanilla in a sauce pan. Melt together over medium high heat. Drizzle over the apples. Bake at 400 degrees for 25-30 minutes.

Eggnog Cheesecake

3, 8 ounce packages cream
cheese, softened

1 cup white sugar

3 tablespoons flour

3/4 cup eggnog

2 eggs

2 tablespoons rum (optional)

1 tablespoon vanilla

1 spoon swirl nutmeg
essential oil*

1 spoon swirl cinnamon
essential oil

Preheat oven to 425 degrees.
In a food processor, combine
cream cheese, sugar, flour and
eggnog; process until smooth.
Blend in eggs, nutmeg and
cinnamon essential oil. Pour
mixture into spring-form pan.

Bake in preheated oven for 10 minutes
Reduce heat to 250 degrees and bake
for 45 minutes, or until center of cake
is barely firm to the touch.

Remove from the oven and
immediately loosen the cake from the
rim. Let cake cool completely before
removing the rim. Can be made the
day ahead and stored in the
refrigerator. Remove one hour prior to
serving.

*See introduction page for delivery
method.

Orange Olive Oil Cake

1 1/4 cups extra virgin olive oil

1 cup sugar

2 cups flour

1/3 cup almond flour or finely ground
   cornmeal

2 teaspoons baking powder

1/2 teaspoon baking soda

1/2 teaspoon kosher salt

3 tablespoons Grand Marnier

2 drops orange essential oil

3 tablespoons fresh lemon juice

2 teaspoons vanilla extract

3 large eggs

Preheat oven to 400 degrees. Spray Bundt pan with non-stick spray. Whisk cake flour, almond flour, baking powder, baking soda, and salt in a medium bowl to combine and eliminate any lumps.

In a separate small bowl, stir together Grand Marnier, orange essential oil, lemon juice, and vanilla. Using an electric mixer on high speed, beat eggs and sugar in a large bowl until mixture is very light, thick, pale, and falls off the whisk or beaters in a slowly dissolving ribbon, about 3 minutes if using a stand mixer and about 5 minutes if using a hand mixer.

With mixer still on high speed, gradually stream in olive oil and beat until mixed thoroughly. Reduce mixer speed to low and add dry ingredients in 3 additions, alternating with Grand Marnier mixture in 2 additions, beginning and ending with dry ingredients.

Scrape batter into prepared pan, smooth top, and sprinkle with more sugar.

Place cake in oven and *immediately reduce oven temperature to 350°*. Bake until top is golden brown, center is firm to the touch, and a tester inserted into the center comes out clean, 40–50 minutes. Transfer pan to a wire rack and let cake cool in pan 15 minutes.

Poke holes all over top of cake with a toothpick or skewer and drizzle with 2 tablespoons oil; let it absorb. Run a thin knife around edges of cake and remove ring from pan. Slide cake onto rack and let cool completely.

Lemon Chiffon Pie

1 large package cook and serve
   lemon pudding mix

8 ounces cream cheese, cubed

1 drop lemon essential oil

2 large containers of Cool Whip

1 frozen pie crust

Bake pie crust according to package directions. Let cool.

Prepare the lemon pudding according to the package directions. Remove from heat. Stir lemon essential oil and cubed cream cheese into the pudding until cream cheese is completely melted. Let cool for approximately 30 minutes, stirring occasionally. Stir in 1 1/2 cups Cool Whip.

Pour the lemon pudding mixture into the cooked pie crust and place in the refrigerator until cool. Top generously with remaining Cool Whip.

Pear Pound Cake

1/2 cup butter, melted

1/2 cup sugar

3 eggs

1/2 teaspoon vanilla

1 cup flour

1 drop lemon essential oil

6 pears, seeded, peeled and cut
   in half

Preheat the oven to 375 degrees. Melt the butter. Add the vanilla and lemon essential oil to the melted butter and mix well. Mix in the sugar and eggs. Add the flour to the mixture and mix well.

Spray a round cake pan with a non-stick spray. Pour in the batter and spread until even. Press the halved pears into the batter, round side down, until the batter is surrounding the pears. Bake for 35 minutes.

Made in the USA
San Bernardino, CA
24 November 2019